5.50

J
SCH

12,913

Schlein, Miriam
    I hate it; pictures by Judith Gwyn Brown.   Albert Whitman
ᶜ1978

    unp   col illus   (Self-starter books)

    Children identify situations that make them feel negative.

    1 Emotions   I Brown, Judith Gwyn, illus.   II Title

                                                                    E; 152.4

I HATE IT

By Miriam Schlein

Pictures by Judith Gwyn Brown

Albert Whitman & Company, Chicago

Also by Miriam Schlein: The Way Mothers Are

Text © 1978 by Miriam Schlein
Illustrations © 1978 by Judith Gwyn Brown
Published simultaneously in Canada
by George J. McLeod, Limited, Toronto
All rights reserved. Printed in U.S.A.

•

Library of Congress Cataloging in Publication Data

Schlein, Miriam.
   I hate it.

   (Self-starter books)
   SUMMARY: *Children identify situations that make*
them feel negative.
      1.   Hate—Juvenile literature.   [1.   Emotions]
I.   Brown, Judith Gwyn.   II.   Title.
BF575.H3S35
ISBN 0-8075-3505-2   152.4   78-1744

I HATE IT

Oh, I hate it when —

—my ice cream falls down.

I hate to get all dressed up.

I don't like it when the snow melts.

I didn't like it when my best friend
moved away.

I hated that . . .

I don't like dogs
that are bigger than
I am . . .

except when they're sitting down.

I don't like it when people invite me,
then change their minds—

No...

It's OK not to like some things.
I don't like it when I get ducked under water.

I hate that!

What kind of things
    happen to you
        that you don't like?

I don't like it when somebody grabs my car.

I don't like to feel cold—

But I don't like it
when I have to wear so much

that I can't move.

I don't like it when my mother cries.

I don't like it when I fall and scrape my knee.

I don't like it when I feel gloomy.

I don't like it when someone gets very bossy.

I really hate it!

But things like that don't happen all the time.
They just happen sometimes...
now and then.

And besides... after a while
my knee gets all better
and more snow falls.

<u>All</u> dogs are not too big,
and I make new friends,
 even though sometimes I still think about
  my good old friend who moved away.

Most of the time
my mother is busy
and funny and happy,

and most of the time when people invite you,
they really <u>do</u> mean it.

Most days
I would say things
are really OK.